SNAPSHOTS IN HISTORY

HURRICANE KATRINA

Aftermath of Disaster

by Barb Palser

HURRICANE KATRINA

Aftermath of Disaster

by Barb Palser

Content Adviser: Michael Perlstein, Staff Writer,
The Times-Picayune, New Orleans

Reading Adviser: Katie Van Sluys, Ph.D.,
School of Education, DePaul University

COMPASS POINT BOOKS
MINNEAPOLIS, MINNESOTA

COMPASS POINT BOOKS

3109 West 50th Street, #115
Minneapolis, MN 55410

Visit Compass Point Books on the Internet at
www.compasspointbooks.com
or e-mail your request to
custserv@compasspointbooks.com

For Compass Point Books
Jennifer VanVoorst, Jaime Martens, XNR Productions, Inc.,
Catherine Neitge, Keith Griffin, and Carol Jones

For Red Line Editorial, Inc.
Bob Temple, Jennifer Lindner, Nadia Higgins, and Lindaanne Donohoe

Library of Congress Cataloging-in-Publication Data
Palser, Barb.
  Hurricane Katrina : aftermath of disaster / by Barb Palser.
      p. cm. — (Snapshots in history)
  Includes bibliographical references and index.
  ISBN-13: 978-0-7565-2101-1 (hardcover)
  ISBN-10: 0-7565-2101-7 (hardcover)
  1. Hurricane Katrina, 2005—Juvenile literature. 2. Hurricanes—
Louisiana—New Orleans—Juvenile literature. 3. Hurricanes—
Gulf Coast (U.S.)—Juvenile literature. 4. Disaster relief—Louisiana
—New Orleans—Juvenile literature. 5. Disaster relief—Gulf
Coast (U.S.)—Juvenile literature. I. Title. II. Series.
  HV6362005.L8 P35 2007
  976'.044—dc22   2006009119

CONTENTS

Shelter of Last Resort

Chapter 1

On Sunday, August 28, 2005, 39-year-old Currise Taylor stood in a long line outside the Superdome sports stadium in New Orleans, Louisiana. She pushed a cart containing medicine, disinfectant, a Butterball turkey, sandwich bread, and a few changes of clothes.

Hipolito Valdez, 62, carried a towel, a mobile phone, and a case for his glasses. Vernell Phillips, 59, had nothing but his watch, his wallet, and the clothes on his back. Joey Branson, 42, had a freshly baked apple pie and a mystery novel. He told a reporter, "That's all I need. I'm set for the duration."

Other people carried blankets, pillows, and hastily packed plastic bags of clothing. They pulled suitcases and coolers. Some had folding tables and chairs. The children clutched toys and snacks.

As Hurricane Katrina approached New Orleans, most residents left the city. Thousands of those who could not leave lined up to get inside the Superdome. The sports stadium operated as a shelter during the crisis.

The thousands of people waiting to get into the Superdome had been told to pack enough food to last a few days. Once they got inside, they might be stuck there for a while. A hurricane was coming.

The 77,000-seat stadium had been designated a hurricane "shelter of last resort" by New Orleans officials. While most city residents had fled the fast-approaching Hurricane Katrina, around 20 percent of the population—100,000 people—were left behind. Many of these people were too weak, too poor, or too old to find a way out of town. They didn't own cars and couldn't afford bus or train tickets. While the rest of the city's residents jammed the highways, the disadvantaged headed for shelters and hoped for the best.

Not all of the people converging on the Superdome were poor, however. Some were tourists who had nowhere else to go. Neil Coffey, 35, was visiting from Britain. He said:

> *When you are on a holiday you don't really follow these kind of things. We were surprised. We don't get hurricanes like this at home.*

Other people came to the Superdome because they had children or elderly relatives to protect. Michael Bivens, 53, brought his wife, daughter, and five young granddaughters. He said:

> *I had to come. Not for me. I ride these out all the time. But I knew I couldn't save those children in this one if something happened.*

Families brought many personal items with them to the Superdome, since they did not know how long they would be away from home.

11

Whatever their reasons for being there, approximately 10,000 people ended up at the Superdome the day before Hurricane Katrina struck. Each person was checked for weapons by National Guard troops before being allowed to enter the building. On the way in, they were given bottles of water and MREs, or "meals ready to eat," by the military. The meals came in sturdy plastic packets.

Once inside, families quickly looked for open places to set up camp. They tried to make themselves comfortable in the stadium seats. They passed the time playing cards and reading books and magazines. The children ran in circles and played; their parents made sure to keep them close. All things considered, the first evening was bearable. The glaring lights were always on and there was a lot of noise, but people had food to eat and there was some sense of order. Anice Sexton, 82, said she'd been treated well:

> *People are so nice, and the people staying here have been really cooperative. But the washrooms are terrible.*

Terry Ebbert, New Orleans' homeland security director, knew the worst was yet to come. Power and water would probably be cut off, and the smells and heat would be sickening. He said:

> *It's going to be very uncomfortable. But that's not why we're here. We're here to make sure that on Tuesday, people are still alive.*

Not even Ebbert imagined how desperate things would get. Early the next morning—Monday, August 29—the families huddled in the Superdome understood how terrible the storm was when they heard the fierce winds and rain roaring outside. Soon the winds tore two large pieces of metal off of the Superdome's roof, and rain started pouring in. However, there was still a sense of hope that the storm would pass and people could return to their homes to survey the hurricane damage, as they had always done after previous storms.

Winds as fast as 140 miles (224 kilometers) per hour tore off parts of the metal covering the Superdome's roof.

Then came the piece of news that changed everything: The levees protecting New Orleans had been overwhelmed by the storm. Water was pouring over and through the broken barriers, flooding into the city. Life would not be normal for a very long time.

In New Orleans, helicopters dropped sandbags into areas flooded by the broken levees. The giant sandbags were meant to fill the gaps in the damaged levees, keeping the flood from spreading.

If the levees in New Orleans had not broken, Hurricane Katrina would be a very different story. It would still have gone down in history as one of the deadliest, costliest, most intense storms ever to hit the United States. It would still have been remembered for the lives that were lost and the towns that were destroyed along the coasts of Louisiana and Mississippi. But the storm itself would have been the main story.

On Monday, August 29, however, four New Orleans levees were overwhelmed, unleashing what many feel was the cause of one of the most horrific humanitarian crises the United States has ever seen. The entire world watched the city fill with murky water while official blunders delayed food, water, and rescue workers from reaching tens of thousands of stranded people. Many of the people who suffered most were elderly, poor, and black. Hurricane Katrina became a story of social and racial division; monumental failures in emergency planning, coordination, and execution at every level of government; and the near-devastation of one of America's most celebrated cities. ◢

FLOOD BARRIERS

Levees are high banks of earth that keep a lake or river from overflowing. Levees can occur naturally, but they are also built by people to protect against flooding. French settlers started building levees around New Orleans in the 1700s. The earthen levees that protect New Orleans today are around 16 feet (4.9 meters) high. Many were built in the 1960s as a response to the flooding caused by Hurricane Betsy.

Gambling Against Nature

Chapter

2

It was no surprise to anyone that a powerful hurricane put the city of New Orleans under water. Not only was Hurricane Katrina one of the worst natural disasters in U.S. history, it was also one of the most accurately predicted.

In the 153 years from 1851 to 2004, 49 hurricanes made landfall on the Louisiana coast. Eighteen of those were classified as major storms by the National Weather Service. The odds of a direct hit to a specific city such as New Orleans were low, but still inevitable. In 2004, University of New Orleans geologist Shea Penland warned:

It's not if it will happen. It's when.

Experts also knew that when the "big one" hit, the outcome would be catastrophic because of the unusual geography around New Orleans. It's hard to imagine a worse place for a hurricane to strike.

When people think of hurricanes, they often picture the huge cyclone of high-speed winds and torrential rains that shatter windows, blow roofs off of buildings, and pull trees out of the ground. However, the greatest damage is often caused by the powerful surge of water a hurricane creates when it comes close to land. The most intense hurricanes can push ashore surges as high as 30 feet (9 m), smashing buildings and flooding entire cities. In areas that are above sea level, gravity drains the water from a storm surge back toward the sea. But most of New Orleans is below sea level.

Trees were uprooted and lifted by Hurricane Katrina.

Imagine an empty bowl sitting in a pool of water that reaches almost to its rim. As long as the water is calm, the bowl will remain empty. But if you were to raise the water level or slosh it around, it would spill into the bowl and stay there.

That is almost exactly the situation in New Orleans. The city is bordered by the 630-square-mile (1,638-square-kilometer) Lake Pontchartrain to the north, with the Mississippi River winding around the south. Along the lake and the river, sea walls and man-made earthen barriers called levees act like the rim of a bowl. If the levees were to break or if water was pushed over them, most of the city would flood, and the water would be trapped inside the bowl. There are canals and pumps to help drain flood waters, but they would be no match for a citywide flood.

Although the levees offer crucial protection against flooding, scientists believe they also make New Orleans more vulnerable to hurricanes. Most people think of floods as destructive events, but they are also constructive. Floods build up the earth by depositing soil in flooded areas. Because

LOUISIANA'S STORMY PAST

The last hurricane to cause major damage in New Orleans was Hurricane Betsy in 1965. Much of the city was flooded, and 58 people in Louisiana died. The deadliest storm to hit Louisiana in recent history was Hurricane Audrey in 1957. Audrey crashed into southern Louisiana, destroying the town of Cameron and killing between 400 and 550 people. In 1893, an unnamed hurricane killed more than 800 people in a small coastal settlement called Cheniere Caminada.

of the prevention of floods and therefore the lack of new soil floods leave behind, the earth around New Orleans is sinking at a rate of 3 feet (90 centimeters) every 100 years. The bowl is getting deeper.

The absence of soil deposits has also contributed to the rapid erosion of marshes and small islands along the Gulf of Mexico. In addition to providing a home for many animal species and supporting a large fishing industry, the wetlands are a natural hurricane barrier. Over open water, hurricane winds move at high speeds and with great force, but when they hit land, they quickly slow down and lose energy. With less marsh area to slow them down, hurricanes can hit land with much greater force and higher surges of water. The oil and gas industries have also contributed to the loss of wetlands by carving canals and building pipelines through the marshes, turning them into open water.

A damaged platform rested at an oil refinery south of Venice, Louisiana.

19

Years before Katrina hit, experts had started to question whether the levees along Lake Pontchartrain were high enough to withstand a major storm surge. When the Army Corps of Engineers set height requirements for the levees in the 1960s, it had rough measurement tools and limited knowledge compared with the high-tech instruments and computer-based forecasting programs we have today. And even if their original measurements were correct, the environment itself had changed over time.

Sinking land, rising sea levels, the erosion of natural barriers, possible weaknesses in the levee system—all of the factors that would make a hurricane especially devastating to New Orleans— had been discussed for decades before Hurricane Katrina hit. In early 2001, the Federal Emergency Management Agency (FEMA) issued a report saying that a hurricane striking New Orleans was one of the three most likely catastrophic disasters in the United States, along with a terrorist attack on New York City and a major earthquake in San Francisco.

DOOMSDAY PREDICTIONS IGNORED

In 2002, *The Times-Picayune* newspaper in New Orleans published an in-depth report, "Washing Away," on the region's vulnerability to hurricanes:

If enough water from Lake Pontchartrain topped the levee system along its south shore, the result would be apocalyptic. Vast areas would be submerged for days or weeks. ... Some places on the east bank of Orleans and Jefferson parishes are as low as 10 feet below sea level.

Whoever remained in the city would be at grave risk. Tens of thousands more would be stranded on rooftops and high ground, awaiting rescue that could take days or longer. They would face thirst, hunger and exposure to toxic chemicals.

In 1998, a group of scientists, engineers, and state officials developed an ambitious plan, called Coast 2050, to restore the region's levees and wetlands. However, the plan's estimated cost was $14 billion, and the group was unable to secure federal funding. In August 2005, just weeks before Hurricane Katrina struck, Congress approved $540 million over four years for coastal restoration in Louisiana.

Knowing the risks, why did people choose to stay in such a dangerous place? Many could not have imagined living anywhere else. South Louisiana is an area with a rich cultural heritage, where family roots go back for generations upon generations—and where families have weathered hurricane after hurricane.

Street musicians performed in New Orleans' French Quarter. Founded in 1718 by French settlers, this historic area is one of the oldest neighborhoods in the United States.

New Orleans' historic French Quarter is a popular tourist destination.

Even for those who weren't native to Louisiana, New Orleans offered an atmosphere unlike that of any other city. Famed as the birthplace of jazz and for its annual Mardi Gras celebration, with the colorful French Quarter as its centerpiece, New Orleans drew visitors from all over the world—some of whom settled down and stayed. Before Hurricane Katrina, tourism brought more than $5 billion each year to the city known as the "Big Easy."

The "Big Easy"

There are various explanations for how New Orleans came to be nicknamed the "Big Easy." Some people believe the name came from a popular dance hall in the early 1900s called Big Easy. There may also have been a style of dance at the time known as Big Easy. Some historians say the name was invented by jazz musicians, because it was so easy for them to find work in the city. More recently, people associated the Big Easy with the slower, more laid-back pace of life of many local residents.

One reason so many people live along the Gulf Coast—or in earthquake zones like San Francisco or in the "Tornado Alley" of the Midwest—is that people gamble against natural disaster all the time. Total destruction is so hard to imagine that the risk is often forgotten in the normalcy of daily life. Most places are vulnerable to some kind of natural disaster, but the danger may not feel real until the disaster actually happens.

On August 29, 2005, it happened.

23

Landfall

3

Residents of coastal Mississippi and Louisiana knew three days in advance that Hurricane Katrina was headed toward them. The storm started as a tropical depression in the Bahamas on August 23, 2005, and quickly moved west, crossing the tip of Florida as a full-fledged hurricane on August 25. By August 26, Katrina was moving across the Gulf of Mexico toward Mississippi and Louisiana. Katrina was still only a Category 2 storm on a scale of 1 to 5, but it was growing stronger by the hour.

It was too early to know where Hurricane Katrina would go or how strong it would become. Still, the region started bracing for a hit. Louisiana Governor Kathleen Blanco declared a state of emergency. Ten thousand National Guard troops were dispatched across the Gulf

Coast. Residents stocked up on drinking water, food, and other emergency supplies. Some made plans to leave town. Others decided to wait before taking any drastic measures. After all, hurricanes are common in the Gulf, and storms often change direction or weaken before reaching land.

Photographed by a pilot one day before the hurricane hit the Gulf Coast, a wall of clouds surrounds the clear eye, or center, of Hurricane Katrina.

On Saturday, August 27, Katrina was a Category 3 hurricane with top winds of 115 miles (184 km) per hour. Mississippi Governor Haley Barbour declared a state of emergency in his state, and New Orleans Mayor Ray Nagin declared a state of emergency in the city. Residents in low-lying areas were told to evacuate. Long lines formed at gas stations, and traffic on highways slowed to a crawl as people fled the region. That evening, the eye of the storm was still 380 miles (608 km) away from the Gulf Coast.

By Sunday, August 28, Katrina had grown into a Category 5 storm. Its top winds reached 175 miles (280 km) per hour, and it was barreling straight toward New Orleans. There was no longer any doubt that big trouble was coming. Mayor Nagin ordered the first mandatory evacuation in New Orleans' history:

> *We are facing a storm that most of us have feared. I do not want to create panic but I do want the citizens to understand that this is very serious. This is a once-in-a-lifetime event.*

Eighty percent of the city's 480,000 residents left before Hurricane Katrina struck. The remaining 100,000 people either refused to leave or could not afford transportation. That was no surprise; earlier studies had predicted that 20 percent of the city's residents would not evacuate. Yet no official action was taken to move the city's poor, elderly, and disabled out of the area before the storm.

PEOPLE STAY WITH PETS

Many people decided not to leave their homes because they refused to leave their pets. Most hurricane shelters did not allow animals. A study in 1997 showed that people without pets are more likely to evacuate for floods or other emergencies than people with pets. After Hurricane Katrina, some citizens and lawmakers campaigned for new rules to require shelters to accept animals.

Instead, 10 shelters were set up as "refuges of last resort" for residents who could not get out of the city. About 10,000 people made their way to the main shelter, the Superdome sports stadium. The National Guard had stocked the Superdome with enough food and water to sustain 15,000 people for three days.

As seen from space, Hurricane Katrina was a mass of clouds swirling around its eye, or center.

SAFFIR-SIMPSON SCALE

The Saffir-Simpson Hurricane Scale is a 1–5 rating that indicates a hurricane's strength, with wind speed as the main factor. The scale was created in 1969 by engineer Herbert Saffir and Robert Simpson, who was director of the National Hurricane Center at the time.

Category 1: Winds 74–95 mph (119–153 kph)

Category 2: Winds 96–110 mph (154–177 kph)

Category 3: Winds 111–130 mph (178–209 kph)

Category 4: Winds 131–155 mph (210–249 kph)

Category 5: Winds greater than 155 mph (249 kph)

That afternoon, President George W. Bush declared federal states of emergency in Mississippi and Alabama. He declared a major disaster in Louisiana, in anticipation of serious damage.

That night, people across the United States watched satellite images of Katrina's movements on TV and the Internet. Along the Mississippi and Louisiana coasts, people who were still in their homes waited for the crushing impact. Families in the Superdome huddled together and tried to rest during the night, which wasn't easy with the sounds and smells of thousands of other people around them.

Hurricane Katrina came ashore at 6:10 in the morning on Monday, August 29, as a Category 3 hurricane. The relatively calm center of the hurricane, known as the eye, passed over the town of Buras, Louisiana, about 70 miles (112 km) southeast of New Orleans. At landfall, the storm was a strong Category 3 with top winds of 125 miles (200 km) per hour. The National Weather Service later declared that Katrina was the third most intense hurricane to hit the United States since record-keeping started

WARNING OF CATASTROPHE

A bulletin issued by the National Hurricane Center on Sunday, August 28, warned:

Potentially catastrophic Hurricane Katrina headed for the northern Gulf Coast ... Preparations to protect life and property should be completed this evening ...

Coastal storm surge flooding of 18 to 22 feet above normal tide levels ... locally as high as 28 feet ... along with large and dangerous battering waves ... can be expected near and to the east of where the center makes landfall. Some levees in the greater New Orleans area could be overtopped. Significant storm surge flooding will occur elsewhere along the central and northeastern Gulf of Mexico coast.

in 1851. Only an unnamed Labor Day hurricane in 1935 and Hurricane Camille in 1969 were more intense. Hurricane Katrina measured 240 miles (384 km) across as it lashed southeastern Louisiana, the entire Mississippi coastline, and southwestern Alabama. As the hurricane traveled along the coast, the devastation spread. More than 1.3 million homes and businesses in the region lost power.

At about 8:15 that morning, a storm surge filled the Mississippi River Gulf Outlet, a shipping canal commonly known as "Mr. Go." Water from Lake Pontchartrain and the Gulf of Mexico spilled over floodwalls and broke through levees in several places. The Industrial Canal levee, which protects a part of New Orleans called the 9th Ward, gave way,

Some houses in New Orleans' 9th Ward were completely covered by water after a levee broke.

and Lake Pontchartrain started gushing into one of the city's poorest neighborhoods. Soon 40,000 homes in the 9th Ward and St. Bernard Parish were flooded. Later in the day, city officials confirmed that the levee along the 17th Street Canal had also been breached. Then two more levees along the London Avenue Canal failed. What was predicted had come to pass: The bowl was filling up.

Meanwhile, Katrina continued on an easterly track across Mississippi, and a more horrific picture of damage developed.

Along the Mississippi coast, streets and homes were flooded as far as six miles (9.6 km) inland. Thirty people died when an apartment complex collapsed in the coastal town of Biloxi. Gulfport was slammed with a 10-foot-high (3-m-high) surge of water. Floating casinos in both Biloxi and Gulfport were tossed out of the Gulf and piled on the shore like toys.

A 30-foot (9-m) surge of water hit Waveland, Mississippi, practically wiping the small town off the map. At the height of the storm, Gus McKay heard a sound like that of a jet engine outside his house in Waveland. When he turned around, he saw a tornado spin through his back yard. A few seconds later, a wall of water slammed into the house. McKay kicked open a window and swam to safety, carrying his elderly mother with him.

In Alabama, the storm surge pushed up Mobile Bay, temporarily flooding parts of downtown

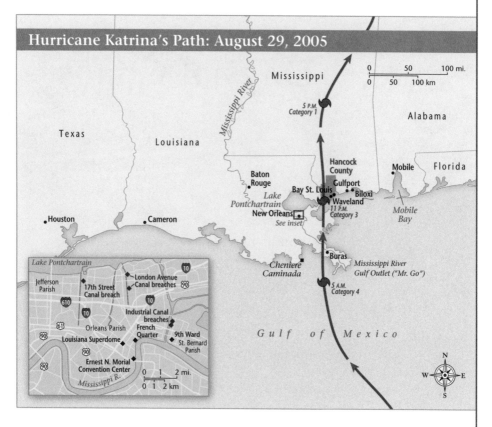

Hurricane Katrina's Path: August 29, 2005

Mississippi

Alabama

Texas

Louisiana

Baton Rouge

Hancock County

Mobile

Florida

Gulfport

Bay St. Louis

Biloxi

Lake Pontchartrain

Waveland

Mobile Bay

New Orleans

See inset

5 P.M. Category 1

11 P.M. Category 3

Houston

Cameron

Cheniere Caminada

Buras

Mississippi River Gulf Outlet ("Mr. Go")

5 A.M. Category 4

Gulf of Mexico

Lake Pontchartrain

Jefferson Parish

17th Street Canal breach

London Avenue Canal breaches

Industrial Canal breaches

Orleans Parish

French Quarter

9th Ward

St. Bernard Parish

Louisiana Superdome

Ernest N. Morial Convention Center

Mississippi R.

0   1   2 mi.
0   1   2 km

N   W   E   S

Mobile in 8 feet (2.4 m) of water. Hurricane Katrina sank or grounded 110 barges, ships, and boats in the Mississippi River and along the coast.

All along the Gulf Coast and in New Orleans, people who had weathered the storm waited for rescue. Many of them were forced to their attics and roofs by rising flood waters. The U.S. Coast Guard started running rescue missions as soon as the storm passed on Monday, but by nightfall thousands remained stranded. Those who were already in shelters grew restless, wondering when they could go home—and what they would find when they got there.

Incredibly, the nightmare was just beginning. ◣

After landfall on August 29, 2005, Hurricane Katrina traveled northward through southern Louisiana and Mississippi.

Days of Chaos

Water levels in New Orleans were still rising swiftly on Tuesday, August 30. Soon 80 percent of the city was under water as deep as 15 feet (4.5 m). Some people swam or waded through chest-deep water to reach higher ground; others were plucked from rooftops by rescue boats and helicopters.

The population in the Superdome quickly rose to more than 20,000. Conditions there went from bad to miserable, with dwindling food and water, a growing stench of waste, and rumors of violence. The building had lost electricity and was running on backup generators, which provided some light but no air conditioning. Soon the Superdome was surrounded by knee-deep water, and there did not appear to be any plan to evacuate the people inside.

Trying to remain cheerful in the face of harsh circumstances, thousands of people rescued from the flood waited to be evacuated from New Orleans. Hundreds of buses ran through the night to bring these people to safe shelter.

The Ernest N. Morial Convention Center became a drop-off location for buses and vans rescuing people from around the city. The Convention Center had not been designated as an official shelter; it had no electricity, no working restrooms, and no food or water.

Soon evacuees were turned away from the overcrowded Superdome and directed toward the Convention Center. Jimmie Fore, the manager of the Convention Center, stood outside and warned people that the facility had no provisions, but with nowhere else to go, they just kept coming.

Electrical lines and phone lines were down across the city, cutting off communication between victims and rescue workers. Before the phones went dead, several thousand 911 calls poured in from flooded and stranded residents, but police were unable to respond because of the chaotic conditions. Recordings of those calls became an eerie reminder of the terror of the early hours of the disaster.

The situation was most urgent in hospitals and nursing homes, where electricity was needed to run medical equipment. A doctor recalled that hospital staff had struggled to keep patients alive in the 110 degree Fahrenheit (43 degree Celsius) heat:

> *We had no electricity. There was no water. It was hot. People are dying. We thought it was as bad as it could get. Why weren't we being evacuated?*

Adding to the confusion and stalling rescue efforts were reports of rampant crime. Fires dotted the landscape; some were believed to be the work

RUMORS DELAY RESCUE

In the days after the storm, rumors of violence in New Orleans spread. While much of the reported violence was real, many stories later turned out to be false. Rescue operations were temporarily halted by reports of gunmen shooting at helicopters. Investigators later confirmed only a single case of shooting at rescue helicopters. They said rescue workers probably heard gunshots and assumed that they were the targets. In some instances, residents in badly flooded neighborhoods fired guns into the air to attract rescuers, and some of this gunfire was mistaken as hostile.

of arsonists. TV cameras caught looters breaking into stores and stealing armloads of clothing and electronics. Soon there were reports of gunmen roaming the passable areas of the city, committing rape and robbery.

About 200 New Orleans police officers failed to show up for duty, stretching resources even thinner. On Wednesday afternoon, Mayor Ray Nagin pulled almost all of the city's police officers off of search-and-rescue duty and ordered them to focus on controlling looting.

After Katrina, New Orleans fell prey to rampant crime and lawlessness. A fire—possibly set by arsonists—burned near the city's center.

35

Why wasn't the city cleared out more quickly? Why were people still waiting for rescue and committing crimes in broad daylight, days after Katrina struck? Where were emergency workers while all of this was going on?

Relief and rescue forces were working hard, but there weren't enough of them. The U.S. Coast Guard started running rescue missions the day the storm struck. National Guard troops from Louisiana, Alabama, and Mississippi were distributing supplies and providing security at shelters.

However, National Guard troops in other states were standing by and waiting for orders. A Navy ship with 600 empty beds and six operating rooms sat in the Gulf of Mexico for several days before receiving orders to help. Volunteers with truckloads of donated supplies were waiting for instructions.

A Hurricane Victim's Personal Account

New Orleans resident Patricia Thompson was one of many flood victims who testified before a congressional committee investigating the response to Hurricane Katrina. On December 6, 2005, she said:

We were abandoned. City officials did nothing to protect us. We were told to go to the Superdome, the Convention Center, the Interstate bridge for safety. We did this more than once. In fact, we tried them all for every day over a week. We saw buses, helicopters and FEMA trucks, but no one stopped to help us. We never felt so cut off in all our lives. We slept next to dead bodies, we slept on streets at least four times next to human feces and urine. There was garbage everywhere in the city. Panic and fear had taken over.

The delays and lack of clear instructions were blamed on confusion and arguments among local, state, and federal authorities. For example, federal officials claimed that Louisiana Governor Kathleen Blanco had not officially requested assistance. According to federal law, the military cannot enter a state to enforce order unless the state's governor makes an official request. Whether Governor Blanco requested federal assistance, and whether she requested it properly, would become issues of great controversy. At one point, President Bush asked Governor Blanco to turn the entire relief effort over to federal control, but Blanco refused to relinquish control of state National Guard troops.

Rescue workers, including those from FEMA and the U.S. Coast Guard, searched by boat for people stranded by the flooding after Hurricane Katrina.

37

In other cases, state and local officials asked for federal help during phone calls, but nothing was done because federal officials were waiting for written requests.

While Mississippi did not experience the level of conflict among government agencies that Louisiana did, there were problems delivering enough supplies where they were needed. In an e-mail message sent September 1, a Mississippi-based official from the Federal Emergency Management Agency (FEMA) warned his superiors that the amounts of ice and water being shipped to Hancock County, Mississippi, were not enough. He said the relief system was broken and that he feared major riots if more ice and water were not sent.

At times it seemed as if the federal government was not aware of how badly the rescue effort in New Orleans was going. In a September 1 television inverview, FEMA director Michael Brown was upbeat about the response:

> *Considering the dire circumstances that we have in New Orleans— virtually a city that has been destroyed ... things are going relatively well.*

FEMA AND DHS

The Federal Emergency Management Agency (FEMA) is the federal agency responsible for responding to national emergencies. In 2003, FEMA became part of the Department of Homeland Security (DHS). The DHS is also in charge of protecting the United States against terrorism. At the time, some people worried that antiterrorism efforts would take DHS resources away from FEMA's emergency-response mission. Those concerns resurfaced after the Hurricane Katrina crisis.

At the local level, however, feelings could not have been more different. In a television interview, Jefferson Parish President Aaron Broussard said:

> *Bureaucracy has committed murder here in the greater New Orleans area. Nobody's coming to get us. Everybody's promised. They've had press conferences. I'm sick of the press conferences.*

On Wednesday, August 31, Governor Blanco announced a plan to transfer the people in the Superdome to the Astrodome sports stadium in Houston, Texas. The first buses departed Wednesday night, and the evacuation continued for three days.

FEMA director Michael Brown looked on as Louisiana Governor Kathleen Blanco addressed reporters at a press conference.

One man waiting in line for a bus to the Astrodome summed up the feelings of Superdome residents:

> *I don't care where they're taking us. Anywhere is better than here.*

By then, New Orleans was believed to be turning into a toxic stew of sewage, household chemicals, pesticides, and gasoline. The bodies of dead people and animals floated in the brown water. People who had died while waiting for rescue were covered with sheets. Pet dogs that had been separated from their owners roamed the streets, disoriented and hungry. Tens of thousands of people were still waiting to be saved.

One sign that suggested top federal officials were out of touch with the situation was their lack of knowledge about evacuees at the Convention Center. By Tuesday, the population at the Convention Center had reached 20,000 and would soon peak at 25,000. Unlike the Superdome, the Convention Center had no system of screening for weapons, no food or water, and almost no police or medical workers.

In an interview with National Public Radio on Thursday, Department of Homeland Security director Michael Chertoff dismissed reports of thousands of people without food or water at the Convention Center as rumors—even though reporters and TV news crews had been on the scene. The same day, FEMA head Brown said on television that the federal government had not even learned

about the situation at the Convention Center until just that day. When Brown repeated that statement on ABC's *Nightline* news show, anchor Ted Koppel was amazed. He asked Brown:

A stray dog roamed the flooded streets of New Orleans' 9th Ward. During the city's evacuation, many pets were left behind.

> *Don't you guys watch television? Don't you listen to the radio?*

Earlier that day, President Bush had publicly praised Brown for his efforts:

> *Brownie, you're doing a heck of a job.*

On Friday, September 2—five days into the crisis—the rescue and recovery effort finally seemed to be moving at full speed. Throughout the day, busloads of evacuees left the Superdome for Houston. A convoy of supplies arrived at the Convention Center. Almost 3,000 stranded patients and doctors were evacuated from Charity and University hospitals. President Bush approved a bill authorizing $10.5 billion to aid those hurt by the hurricane.

On Saturday, the evacuation of the Superdome was completed, and buses began evacuating the Convention Center. President Bush promised to send 7,000 military personnel to the Gulf

FEMA search and rescue workers arrived on boats to move people stranded in flooded areas.

to reinforce the 4,000 troops already there. The Department of Defense sent 10,000 National Guard troops to supplement the 30,000 already there or on the way. On Sunday, cruise ships were sent to the Gulf to serve as temporary housing for evacuees and emergency workers.

Meanwhile, the Army Corps of Engineers rushed to repair the breached levees by dropping giant sandbags into the gaps. A little more than a week after the storm, the levees were patched, and the slow process of pumping water back into Lake Pontchartrain began.

Pumping life back into New Orleans would take a lot longer.

Help at Last

In many ways, the federal government's response to Hurricane Katrina was troubling. Fortunately, the response of individuals, organizations, and governments in other states was fast and enormous. While officials argued over rules and procedure, heroes leapt to action.

Some acts of kindness were small but meaningful. People stranded in the Superdome shared food with others who had nothing to eat and watched each other's children.

Other stories were more dramatic. Roy Henderson used his small boat to save 10 people in Waveland, Mississippi. In Biloxi, Mississippi, 13-year-old Phillip Bullard swam back and forth through a window in his submerged house to save 12 friends and family members. He later said:

> *I just didn't want to see my family drown. I was scared [that] if I didn't keep helping, somebody would die.*

Twenty-year-old Jabbar Gibson stole an abandoned school bus in New Orleans and picked up 70 people as he drove 300 miles (480 km) to Houston. Along the way, his passengers pooled their money to pay for gas. Gibson's bus was the first to arrive at Houston's Astrodome. When Gibson was asked whether he was worried about getting in trouble for stealing the bus, he said:

> *I don't care if I get blamed for it so long as I saved my people. If we had stayed there, we would still have been waiting.*

When Gibson's passengers and the other busloads of evacuees got to Houston, they were met by workers from the American Red Cross. The Astrodome had air conditioning, showers, and working toilets. People were given hot meals, personal hygiene kits, and medical attention. Uniformed police officers were on the scene to maintain order. For thousands of hot, tired, hungry evacuees, the Astrodome offered some relief.

THE AMERICAN RED CROSS

Founded in 1881, the American Red Cross is a nonprofit organization that helps victims of war and natural disasters. No other organization played nearly as great a role in the aftermath of Hurricane Katrina as the Red Cross. The Red Cross operated 1,100 shelters in 27 states for Hurricane Katrina victims, including the shelter at the Astrodome in Houston, Texas. The Red Cross called up 219,000 volunteers to help run the shelters and pass out supplies. Funding for Red Cross efforts comes from individual and corporate donations.

Conditions at the Houston Astrodome in Texas were a major improvement over those at the New Orleans Superdome. Thousands of evacuees from Louisiana stayed at the makeshift shelter.

By Friday morning, September 2, the Astrodome was overflowing with 15,000 storm victims. Houston Mayor Bill White opened a nearby arena called the Reliant Center to take in 11,000 more people. The Texas cities of San Antonio and Dallas each made room for 25,000 people.

Soon Texas' shelters brimmed with nearly 250,000 evacuees. On September 4, Texas Governor Rick Perry ordered that some of those people be moved to other states. Offers came from dozens of states as far away as Michigan, Oregon, and Colorado. Arkansas took in 60,000 evacuees, increasing the total population of the state by 2.5 percent.

However, many evacuees were able to stay close to home. Louisiana's capital city of Baton Rouge

SEVEN CHILDREN ALL ALONE

Rescue workers in New Orleans couldn't believe their eyes: A 6-year-old boy was walking down the road carrying a baby. Five toddlers followed him, some barely old enough to walk. The children were all holding hands and following the boy. How did these children end up alone, with a 6-year-old as their leader?

Three days later, rescue workers found the boy's mother in a shelter in San Antonio, Texas. The mother explained that two of the children were hers, and the five others lived in the same apartment building. They had all been trapped for four days during the flood with no food, light, or air conditioning. And the water kept rising.

When a rescue helicopter arrived, everyone agreed the children should be saved first. The children were dropped off on a highway where other evacuees were gathered. Eventually the adults were rescued by a different helicopter and ended up at a shelter in San Antonio. Thanks to the hard work of rescue workers, the families were reunited.

absorbed more than 200,000 people from around New Orleans. Almost overnight, the population of Baton Rouge grew from 400,000 to 600,000. And in Mississippi, Red Cross shelters housed 17,000 storm victims.

In addition to shelters run by the Red Cross, many people found refuge in small church- and community-run shelters. Many more went to government-paid hotel rooms and the homes of friends, relatives, and generous strangers.

One of the most important things people found in the shelters was a link to the outside world. In the panic of the flood and the chaos of the evacuation, many families had been torn apart. Parents and grandparents were separated from children, and mothers were separated from their babies. When the rescued evacuees were loaded onto buses and airplanes, they usually had no idea where they were being taken until hours into the trip. Friends and relatives had no way to know whether their loved ones were dead or alive.

People outside the Astrodome shelter held up signs in an effort to find missing relatives.

48

As soon as victims were able to reach telephones and the Internet, the tide turned. Almost overnight, dozens of Web sites sprang up to help find missing people. Each Web site was like a "lost and found" center for human beings. People published photographs and information about their loved ones in the hope that someone had seen them. Other people posted messages to let their friends and family know they had survived. Photographs of the missing plastered the walls of shelters. Pictures were shown on television, and names were broadcast on radio stations. Thousands of lost people were found within days. Yet thousands remained missing.

ONLINE CALLS FOR HELP

Thousands of people posted messages on Internet bulletin boards in the days after the storm:

I am looking for my mother and my stepfather. My mother is probably in need of medical help. I do not know if they have been rescued. My stepfather cannot swim and my mother is unable to walk.

Please Help! The last time I heard from my mom she was stranded perhaps trapped inside an apartment in New Orleans East. If she has been rescued please inform her that her five children are OK.

All are OK. Need food and water, ice and gasoline, but everyone survived the storm.

My mother was rescued from her roof Wednesday morning and is now safe in Houston.

Meanwhile, volunteers across the country rushed to help their fellow Americans. Some of them came with official relief organizations; others came on their own. They drove boats into the flood waters to search for stranded victims. They passed out food, water, and clothing. They rescued lost, starving animals.

College students came all the way from Alaska to help with the cleanup after Hurricane Katrina.

A caravan of buses from Minnesota drove a 52-hour, 2,300-mile (3,680-km) round trip to drop off food, water, and diapers to evacuees in Louisiana. Airlines flew people to shelters in faraway cities and states. At FEMA's request, a Colorado ambulance company supplied 130 ambulances to help with evacuation.

Three hundred New York City firefighters traveled to New Orleans to help local firefighters who had worked for days without rest. Louisiana was one of many states that sent firefighters to New York after the terrorist attacks of September 11, 2001. For the

New York firefighters, Hurricane Katrina was a chance to repay the favor. One New York firefighter said:

> *I know that these people were up there to take care of us. We have to help them out when they're in times of peril.*

Other people sent donations of food, supplies, and blood. Churches and private companies raised millions of dollars for storm victims. Even school children collected money for people who needed help. Many donations went to the Red Cross, which had collected more than $1 billion by the end of September. Former presidents George H. W. Bush, a Republican, and Bill Clinton, a Democrat, joined forces to create a fund that received more than $100 million in contributions. A large portion of that money was given to storm-ravaged colleges and universities.

In a September 7 e-mail message to her friends and family, Maria Russell of Bay St. Louis, Mississippi, wrote:

> *Our friends from Knoxville [Tennessee] arrived, not only with a trailerful of supplies, but with the announcement that a television news crew was en route with the sole purpose of focusing on Bay St. Louis. It seems that the media is fixated on New Orleans, Biloxi and Gulfport, but there is little mention of our little town or Waveland. This was the first time I really felt hope.*

Donations also flowed in from other parts of the world. Within a week of the storm, 70 countries had made offers of aid. Ships from Europe arrived at U.S. ports with food and blankets. Even poor countries like Bangladesh pledged large donations of money and supplies. Mexico sent 45 military trucks full of food and medicine. Sri Lanka, still recovering from a tsunami that killed 30,000 people

After Katrina, only the still floodwaters filled the once-busy streets of New Orleans' French Quarter.

in 2004, sent money to help Katrina's victims.

For many foreigners, the images shown on television were a great surprise. They saw dirty shelters overflowing with elderly and poor people. They saw looting and raging fires in the streets and local officials begging for help. None of these scenes matched their image of one of the world's wealthiest and most powerful nations. Robert Hunter, an expert in foreign policy, said that Hurricane Katrina changed the image of the United States in the eyes of the rest of the world:

> *I think there was a sense of shock that the United States was no better prepared than a Third World country.*

AMERICAN REFUGEES?

Many news reports referred to people escaping the flood as "refugees." That decision offended some people, who said the word *refugee* made flood victims seem like foreigners or second-class citizens. The Reverend Jesse Jackson, a prominent black leader, said in a television interview:

We are not refugees. That is racist language. We are American citizens.

Some news organizations quickly stopped using the word *refugee*, choosing to use *evacuee* or *victim* instead. Others defended the decision, saying it was an accurate description of thousands of people who had fled their homes in a major crisis. Dictionaries disagree on whether the term can describe people who have been forced from their homes but not their countries.

In fact, many Americans were also surprised at what they saw. Hurricane Katrina shook Americans' trust in their government to handle a large-scale emergency and to care for those who didn't have the resources to help themselves. ◣

53

No Place Like Home

Chapter

6

For some hurricane victims, the process of cleaning up Katrina's wreckage and rebuilding their lives started within a few weeks. However, many people soon realized it would be months before they could return home. For some it would take years. Many would never go back.

On September 15, Mayor Ray Nagin said that people could return to the less-damaged neighborhoods in New Orleans. Four days later, however, a new tropical storm named Rita moved into the Gulf of Mexico. Once again, everyone was ordered out of New Orleans amid fears that the damaged levees would not protect the city.

On September 24, Hurricane Rita slammed ashore near the Texas-Louisiana border. With the memory of Katrina still fresh, most people had

At times, FEMA search and rescue workers literally carried hurricane victims to safety.

evacuated ahead of the storm, and fewer than 10 deaths were reported. However, the damage to property was severe. Some small towns in eastern Texas and western Louisiana were destroyed. Thousands of cattle from local ranches were killed. Families who were left homeless by Rita joined Katrina's victims in shelters.

In New Orleans, Rita's heavy rains and storm surge poured through weak spots in the patched levees and flooded some neighborhoods a second time. The worst flooding happened in the Lower 9th Ward and neighboring St. Bernard Parish, which had also taken the hardest hits from Katrina.

After Rita passed, the trickle of people into New Orleans started up again. Some were lucky enough to find their homes in livable condition. But many found rubble where their homes had once been. Entire buildings, cars, and boats had vanished.

Even for people with homes to return to, living in the city would be difficult. Electricity, water, and sewer services were still down or unreliable in most of the city. There were few traffic lights or streetlights, and roads were still blocked by debris. For vast distances there were no stores, gas stations, or restaurants. Curfews were strictly enforced in all parts of the city. Checkpoints were set up on all

KINDNESS OF STRANGERS

Many people opened their homes to complete strangers after the hurricanes. Greg Lawrence of Minneapolis, Minnesota, had a brand new house that he had planned to rent out. When he saw a news report about storm victims searching for homes, he decided to help. He invited a family of seven to live in his three-bedroom house for a year without paying rent. KneKeng Robertson, one of the family members who was invited to live in Lawrence's house, was amazed by the kindness of strangers:

I lost everything, but I'm here with my family in a whole other state with people I don't know. They're opening their hearts to us and we have somewhere to call home.

roads leading into New Orleans to ensure that only residents, workers, and other authorized people were allowed in. There was almost no medical care for the sick and elderly, and no schools for the children. New Orleans was a ghost town.

After the levee broke near New Orleans' 9th Ward, floodwaters lifted entire houses off their foundations and carried them several blocks away. Some were destroyed.

The situation in small towns was the same, or worse. Entire towns looked like they had been flattened by a bomb. People had to make a decision: Should they try to survive in the primitive conditions where their homes had been, or should they look for new homes somewhere else?

57

Katrina and Rita victims started moving out of shelters and into temporary homes. Many people moved in with friends and relatives across the country. FEMA paid for tens of thousands of families to stay in hotel rooms and apartments. Four cruise ships were chartered by FEMA to serve as temporary housing.

In total, 770,000 people were displaced by Katrina and Rita. It was the biggest scattering of people in the United States since the great Dust Bowl migrations of the 1930s, when millions of Midwestern farmers abandoned their dried-up lands and moved west toward California.

However, the Dust Bowl migrations took place over a period of years. Katrina's upheaval happened in a matter of weeks.

The displaced families were glad to be out of the shelters, but life was still stressful. They didn't know how long the government would continue to pay for their housing. They had trouble finding jobs. They missed their neighbors and their familiar customs and foods. Some had moved to northern states, where the cold winter weather was an unpleasant surprise. They didn't know whether they would ever be able to move back home.

Some people, however, found opportunity in the situation. Many who lost their homes in New Orleans had lived in poverty before Katrina struck. Others simply liked the idea of a fresh start. One woman who had evacuated to Houston said:

> *This is a whole new beginning, a whole new start. I mean, why pass up a good opportunity, to go back to something that you know has problems?*

For children, new towns also meant new schools, teachers, and classmates. When Katrina struck in late August, the school year was just starting. Schools across the country quickly opened their doors to the displaced students. Many children were able to make new friends, but they still missed their old schools. Some of them felt different and uncomfortable around so many strangers. One girl said:

> *It's kind of like my first-ever day of school, so I don't really have a lot of friends and I don't know any of the teachers.*

Students at Angie Junior High School in New Orleans held a ribbon at the dedication ceremony of two new classroom buildings. Their previous school building, built in 1938, was destroyed by Katrina.

Life was also strange for people who stayed in New Orleans and other storm-ravaged communities. FEMA provided travel trailers and mobile homes for people who wanted to live nearby while they slowly cleaned and repaired their homes. As time went by, more FEMA trailers started appearing in people's yards, and neighbors were reunited. However, the cities still looked like war zones, and there was not much to do except work on cleaning the mess. The children who came home with their parents were sometimes lonely without their old friends and after-school activities.

In one 30-block area of New Orleans' 9th Ward, flooding swept away all of the houses. Remains of the houses lay in piles.

No matter where people went after the storms, their lives were a chaos of phone calls and paperwork. FEMA's telephone hotlines rang without stopping for 176 days after Hurricane Katrina struck. So many people tried to contact relief agencies and insurance companies at the same time that phone lines were jammed, and it took a long time to get a response from anyone. Even finding out when electricity or water would be restored to a particular neighborhood seemed an almost impossible task.

Frustration with the federal government's response was particularly high. FEMA had accomplished a lot in the first weeks after the storm. The agency helped with search-and-rescue operations; directed truckloads of food, water, and ice to affected areas; and rushed medical workers to help hospitals in Louisiana and Mississippi. FEMA was in charge of organizing the work of dozens of federal agencies and distributing billions of dollars in assistance. However, FEMA had never faced such a large disaster before, and some of the agency's plans did not go smoothly.

On September 7, when the shelters were still full, FEMA said it would give debit cards worth $2,000 to Katrina victims. However, FEMA officials at Houston's Astrodome didn't know about the plan and had no cards to offer the people who rushed to claim them. Two days later, after a few thousand cards had been given out, the plan was suddenly canceled.

Over and over, FEMA set deadlines for families to move out of their government-paid hotel rooms, only to extend the deadlines. Then thousands of people living on cruise ships were ordered to leave. Some of those people sued FEMA, claiming the agency had failed to provide alternate housing.

Meanwhile, thousands of FEMA trailers sat empty in "holding zones" for months while storm victims waited for them. FEMA blamed the delay on local officials in Louisiana and federal restrictions on

For many Gulf Coast residents, Hurricane Katrina left them no home to return to.

where trailers could be placed. Congressman Mike Ross of Arkansas, where more than 10,000 trailers sat empty, said the waste was sickening:

> *They are all brand-new, all totally furnished, and yet people have been living in tents for five months in a row. It just makes you sick to your stomach.*

For the families uprooted by the disaster, normal life was still a long way away.

63

Tragedy's Toll

As the floodwaters gradually went down, the extent of the property damage caused by Hurricane Katrina was revealed. It would take much longer for the other effects of the tragedy to be understood.

In the early days of the crisis, rumors and exaggerations were everywhere. A doctor at the Superdome told a television reporter that several murders and rapes had taken place over the course of two days. Another doctor told a colonel with the National Guard that there were 200 bodies at the Superdome. Mayor Ray Nagin said on a television talk show that "hooligans" had killed and raped people.

The national news media were heavily criticized for repeating such stories without making sure they were true. Even though many of those

stories came from people who would normally be very trustworthy, the media were blamed for giving the world a far worse impression of New Orleans than was true.

New Orleans Mayor Ray Nagin and Louisiana Governor Kathleen Blanco spoke to reporters at a press conference.

A week after the storm, Mayor Ray Nagin estimated the death toll in New Orleans would reach 10,000. The number was actually much lower. Six months after Katrina hit, around 1,300 bodies had been recovered. However, the exact number of deaths caused by Hurricane Katrina probably will never be known. Some bodies were washed away or buried deep in the rubble. Other people had simply scattered in the evacuation and had not told anybody where they were.

The words possible body *warned recovery workers that there might be a dead body inside a badly damaged house. Rescue teams with specially trained dogs searched buildings before demolition.*

Of the confirmed deaths, 1,080 were in Louisiana. More than 200 bodies were found in Mississippi. Alabama and Georgia reported two hurricane-related deaths each. The storm was blamed for killing 11 people in Florida before it headed toward the Gulf Coast. In the hardest-hit neighborhoods of New Orleans, bodies were still being found seven months after the storm.

The people who paid the highest price were the elderly. People more than 60 years old made up only 15 percent of the population in the New Orleans area, but accounted for nearly 75 percent of Katrina-related deaths. Twenty percent of the victims were found in nursing homes and hospitals.

In addition to the human loss, countless animals lost their lives in the storm. Volunteers rescued thousands of dogs, cats, and other pets from the floodwaters. Hundreds of pets were reunited with their families, while most were adopted by new owners from all parts of the country. Many others drowned or starved.

Two weeks after the storm, eight dolphins from a New Orleans aquarium were found huddled together in the Gulf of Mexico. The dolphins were rescued, but thousands of other animals in the aquarium died when emergency generators ran out of fuel.

The storm also dealt a huge blow to wildlife in the Gulf region. The violence of Hurricane Katrina killed or drove away many birds, fish, mammals, and reptiles that lived in the coastal wetlands. Saltwater surged into freshwater marshes, and acres of trees farther inland were flattened. People who depended on Louisiana's forestry and fishing industries lost much of their livelihoods.

SUPERDOME DEATHS EXAGGERATED

When workers went to the Superdome and the Convention Center to recover dead bodies, they expected to find dozens or perhaps hundreds of corpses. During the crisis, people had spoken of rampant murder and bodies stacked in freezers. However, only 10 bodies were found at the Superdome, and four were found at the Convention Center. Another 20 were found near the Convention Center. Of those deaths, only one was confirmed as a homicide. One Superdome death was a suicide, another was caused by a drug overdose, and the others were attributed to natural causes.

Fortunately, wildlife recovers quickly from natural disasters like hurricanes. Unfortunately, wildlife and human communities recover more slowly from pollution caused by chemical and oil spills. More than 7 million gallons (27 million liters) of oil were spilled along the Gulf Coast from refineries, broken pipelines, and sunken boats. A damaged oil storage tank spilled more than 800,000 gallons (3 million l) of oil into neighborhoods of St. Bernard Parish. Mixed with the oil were chemicals from industrial plants and bacteria from ruptured sewage systems. Much of the oil was cleaned up within a couple of months, but scientists said the remaining oil and chemicals could affect the ecosystem for decades.

A massive oil spill resulted when an oil tank was lifted off its base by Hurricane Katrina's storm surge.

In New Orleans, people worried about the toll on public health. Buildings that had been flooded

were invaded by mold, which triggered allergic reactions and breathing problems such as asthma. Also, a blanket of contaminated sludge covered the city after the flood. When the sludge dried, it turned into dust, which was easily stirred into the air and inhaled. In addition to serious dangers, the city was also full of unpleasant messes and smells. In one giant dump, 300,000 refrigerators sat waiting to be cleaned of rotten food and crushed for recycling.

NURSING HOME TRAGEDY

One of the most disturbing of Hurricane Katrina's human tragedies was the drowning of 35 people in a nursing home in New Orleans' St. Bernard Parish. The operators of the nursing home had decided not to evacuate the building, even though they were offered assistance by local officials. Later, the operators said they had been afraid that some of their patients were too weak to be moved.

In early December, after three months of testing, officials declared that most of the city was safe to live in. However, some scientists disagreed. They conducted their own tests, which showed dangerous levels of lead and other toxins in the soil. Children are especially vulnerable to lead poisoning, which was already a problem in New Orleans before Katrina. One grandmother who lived in the Lower 9th Ward said she didn't want her granddaughter to visit her until all of the contaminated soil was removed:

You know, we want our children back. We want a safe, sanitary community. Something has got to be done.

Together with Rita, Hurricane Katrina was not only the most destructive natural disaster in U.S. history, but also the most expensive. Some of the obvious costs included rescue and shelter operations, financial aid for victims, and rebuilding property. Other costs were more difficult to measure, such as the loss of jobs and the long-term impact on the oil, fishing, and forestry industries. The costs of property damage alone were estimated to be $100 billion. The exact cost—like the exact death toll—will never be known.

EVIDENCE OF EARLY WARNINGS

Four days after Katrina hit, President Bush said on national television: "I don't think anybody anticipated the breach of the levees." Later, the media published records of meetings that took place in the days before the storm. In those meetings, President Bush and other officials were warned of "grave concerns" that the levees would be breached. Then-FEMA leader Michael Brown also raised concerns about medical care and security at the Superdome, and the strength of the Superdome's roof.

There was also a political price to pay in Katrina's aftermath. On September 9, Michael Brown, the head of FEMA and the man in charge of the federal government's hurricane response, was called back to Washington, D.C. Brown had become the focus of criticism over the government's slow reaction in the first days of the crisis. He resigned from FEMA three days later. Coast Guard Vice Admiral Thad Allen was put in charge of the recovery effort.

However, it was clear that Brown was not the only person to blame. Officials at all levels of government would have to explain why the evacuation and relief efforts went so terribly wrong. ◧

After FEMA director Michael Brown left the recovery effort, Coast Guard Vice Admiral Thad Allen (left) was put in charge of cleaning up after Katrina.

Rebirth

In February 2006, New Orleans marked a milestone by celebrating its first Mardi Gras after Hurricane Katrina.

People dressed in wild costumes and paraded through the streets for days. Tourists came to join the celebration and look around. The Convention Center, which had been a scene of tragedy just months before, hosted parties once again. The historic French Quarter was on higher ground than many parts of the city and had escaped major damage. The spirit of the Big Easy was still alive.

However, no party could be big enough to make people forget that most of New Orleans was still a wasteland. Six months after Katrina struck, fewer than 200,000 people were living in the city.

People in Mardi Gras costumes paraded through the streets of New Orleans in February 2006.

New Orleans' population before Katrina had been 480,000. In St. Bernard Parish, one of the worst-flooded areas, only 10 percent of residents had been able to come back home.

In Mississippi, more than 33,000 families were still living in FEMA trailers, and they were the lucky ones. Others were still living in military-style tents and waiting for their trailers to arrive.

Debris was still being cleared away all along the coast. There was still no water or power in some neighborhoods. People were still stripping moldy carpet from their homes and waiting for insurance money. Crushed roofs were covered with blue tarps for temporary protection. Many families with children couldn't move back because not enough schools were open. And the Army Corps of Engineers was racing to repair miles of damaged levees before the next hurricane season.

WHAT IS MARDI GRAS?

Mardi Gras is the last day of Carnival, a two-week celebration that includes feasts, parades, and lavish parties. Mardi Gras always falls on the Tuesday before Ash Wednesday, which marks the start of the Christian season of Lent. Carnival is seen as a last chance for indulgence before the fasting and sacrifice of Lent begins. Carnival is celebrated around the world, but nowhere in the United States are the celebrations more extravagant than in New Orleans. For many Americans, Mardi Gras is synonymous with New Orleans.

Meanwhile, officials were investigating what had gone wrong with the government's response. One reason for the investigations was to hold people accountable for mistakes that had been made. Another reason was to avoid making the same mistakes in the next major crisis.

Little by little, the victims of Hurricane Katrina began rebuilding their homes — and their lives.

75

President George W. Bush reaffirmed his commitment to assist those affected by Hurricane Katrina at a visit with Louisiana Governor Kathleen Blanco and Coast Guard Vice Admiral Thad Allen.

In February 2006, a report was published by a committee of Republicans in the U.S. House of Representatives. The report, titled "A Failure of Initiative," was highly critical of President Bush, Homeland Security Director Michael Chertoff, and other senior officials. The committee said Chertoff was late in activating the government's emergency response systems, which delayed the arrival of federal troops and supplies. Instead of waiting for local officials to make formal requests for assistance, the report said, the federal government should have responded immediately. Chertoff was also criticized for putting the untrained Michael Brown in charge of FEMA's response.

As for President Bush, the committee said the response might have been faster if he had been involved earlier. Only the president, the report said, has the power to unite federal forces quickly during a crisis.

Finally, the report criticized Louisiana Governor Kathleen Blanco and New Orleans Mayor Ray Nagin for failing to evacuate the city's poor and disabled. The report read:

> *The failure to order timely mandatory evacuations, Mayor Nagin's decision to shelter but not evacuate the remaining population, and decisions of individuals led to an incomplete evacuation. The incomplete pre-landfall evacuation led to deaths, thousands of dangerous rescues, and horrible conditions for those who remained.*

RAISING ISSUES OF RACE

While many people blamed the sluggish relief effort on bad government planning, others believed racism was a factor. In a public opinion survey taken a week after Hurricane Katrina struck, 66 percent of black Americans said the government response would have been faster if most of the victims had been white. Only 17 percent of white Americans agreed with that statement.

Whether or not racism was a direct factor in the rescue effort, political leaders of different races agreed that long-standing problems of discrimination and poverty had resulted in terrible suffering for those citizens who were poor, black, and elderly.

In a speech, Democratic National Committee Chairman Howard Dean said:

We have come to terms with the ugly truth that skin color, age and economics played a significant role in who survived and who did not. And this question, 40 and 50 years after Dr. [Martin Luther] King [Jr.] and the civil rights movement, is, "How could this still be happening in America?"

The White House also conducted an internal review of the response to Katrina. The White House report did not blame specific leaders for the breakdown in organization. Instead, it focused on the need to fix confusing bureaucratic regulations. Homeland Security Adviser Frances Townsend explained it this way:

> *Unfortunately, the one thing that the government tends to be the best at is red tape. But what we know is when we're fighting a deadly hurricane or a terrorist threat, red tape can no longer be tolerated or accepted.*

The report, "The Federal Response to Hurricane Katrina: Lessons Learned," suggested 125 changes to improve emergency response. They included:

- Establishing better coordination and communication among federal, state, and local authorities.

- Relying on federal troops to step in more quickly when state and local responders are overwhelmed.

- Storing key emergency supplies at regional centers for faster delivery to disaster areas.

- Creating a more reliable communication system so that important information can be shared immediately.

While the federal government was worrying about the next national crisis, people along the Gulf Coast were focused on a specific question: Would they be ready for the next hurricane?

In the aftermath of Katrina, some people suggested that New Orleans should not be rebuilt. They pointed to high rates of crime and poverty before Katrina and asked whether the city was worth rebuilding. They also wondered how long it would be before the city was under water again. One science professor said:

> *New Orleans naturally wants to be a lake. A city should never have been built there in the first place.*

Floodwaters turned the streets of downtown New Orleans into rivers after Hurricane Katrina.

For residents and people who loved the city, however, abandoning New Orleans was out of the question. Two weeks after the storm, Governor Blanco promised:

> *To anyone who suggests this great city should not be rebuilt, we will rebuild.*

A commission in New Orleans said rebuilding should be delayed for four months in the hardest-hit areas. The commission said time was needed to study the safety of living in those areas. Mayor Nagin disagreed; he said homeowners had a right to rebuild wherever they wanted.

Volunteers from across the country pitched in to build new houses for Hurricane Katrina victims.

Many people started rebuilding their flooded homes, including those in low-lying areas and near failed levees. Experts urged people to raise their homes off the ground to protect against another flood, but many saw that advice as unrealistic. Many residents could not afford the money or the time it would take to raise a house off the ground. Rebuilding with no extra protection might seem like a huge risk, but as a disaster expert explained, people don't always think about risks rationally:

> *After a disaster, people want to get back to normalcy as quickly as possible—even if it flies in the face of what outsiders would consider rational.*

Some people also showed a lot of confidence in the levees to protect against another catastrophic flood. One homeowner said:

> *Once they're rebuilt, I'm not concerned they'll break again.*

Scientists weren't as confident. Already there was criticism about how the levees were being reconstructed. Furthermore, the height requirements for levees and floodwalls were set in 1959, and those levees were only built to withstand a slow-moving Category 3 storm. Conditions were much different by 2006, and engineers warned that the levees should be higher.

Community leaders were not only eager to rebuild; they wanted to build better towns and cities than they'd had before. In New Orleans, city leaders talked about creating new public parks in some of the low-lying areas. They wanted to improve the way the levee system was managed. They hoped to gain control over the city's high crime rate. And they saw an opportunity to fix the school system, which had serious problems before Katrina struck. For decades, the New Orleans school district had been plagued by poor performance, corruption, and theft. Many of the school buildings that were damaged by the hurricane had already been crumbling in disrepair. Some leaders talked about building new types of schools that would include community programs and much better environments for students.

The same kind of talk was happening along Mississippi's Gulf Coast, where city leaders spoke of

rebuilding more beautiful towns and cities. Mississippi Governor Haley Barbour told the state legislature:

> In 30 years, when I'm dead and gone, people will look at what the coast and South Mississippi have become. If it is simply a newer version of today, we will have failed those people—our children and grandchildren.

Pamela Blanchard, a "Teacher of the Year" at Angie Junior High School in New Orleans, helped one of her sixth-grade students with a reading lesson in a new classroom provided by FEMA.

Rebuilding towns and levees would be a big job, but an even bigger challenge remained: Louisiana's coast was still eroding, and New Orleans was still sinking. In fact, hurricanes Katrina and Rita had wiped away another 100 square miles (260 sq km) of wetlands. For people to continue to live in the region, they would have to either build ever-stronger defenses against nature or figure out how to reverse the impact of human activity.

Finally, the worst natural disaster in U.S. history was a rallying cry for social change. Poverty and racism were unpleasant problems that were often not discussed by individual citizens, politicians, and the media. John Edwards, the 2004 Democratic vice presidential candidate, said in a television interview:

> *One of the things that I hope we will do is look at this as an opportunity ... to shine a bright light on poverty in America and do something about it nationally.*

When Hurricane Katrina crashed into the Gulf Coast in August 2005, many things were exposed. The storm's victims were overwhelmingly poor, black, and elderly. The disaster forced people to think about poverty and racial division in American cities. It uncovered serious flaws in disaster planning at all levels of government. It reminded people that nature has the power to both protect and destroy. It also produced thousands of stories of human kindness, as people banded together and risked their lives

to save strangers. Hurricane Katrina began as a tropical depression in the Bahamas, but it ended as a lesson for the entire nation. ◣

People walked through the New Orleans floodwaters to get to higher ground.

Timeline

August 23, 2005

The 12th tropical depression of the 2005 hurricane season forms over the Bahamas.

August 24, 2005

The depression is now Tropical Storm Katrina, headed for Florida.

August 25, 2005

Katrina becomes a hurricane and kills 11 people in South Florida.

August 26, 2005

Katrina crosses Florida and enters the Gulf of Mexico, heading for Louisiana as a Category 2 hurricane; Louisiana governor declares state of emergency.

August 27, 2005

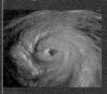

Katrina is a Category 3 hurricane; residents evacuate coastal Louisiana and Mississippi; Mississippi governor declares state of emergency.

August 28, 2005

Now a Category 5 hurricane, Katrina is headed straight for New Orleans, Louisiana; residents who cannot leave are told to go to shelters; Alabama governor declares state of emergency.

August 29, 2005

6:10 A.M.: Katrina makes landfall as a Category 3 hurricane with top winds of 125 miles (200 km) per hour.

8:15 A.M.: The Mississippi River Gulf Outlet and the Industrial Canal levee in New Orleans give way; water pours into St. Bernard Parish and the Lower 9th Ward.

9 A.M.: Katrina moves over the Louisiana-Mississippi border, destroying everything in its path.

9:30 A.M.: Winds tear two holes in the roof of the Superdome, where 10,000 people are sheltered.

12–5 P.M.: Levees along New Orleans' 17th Street Canal and London Avenue Canal are breached; flooding grows steadily worse.

August 30, 2005

Eighty percent of New Orleans is under water; the Superdome population rises to 20,000; fires and looting break out around the city.

August 31, 2005

Conditions worsen for evacuees in the Superdome and Convention Center due to lack of power, sanitation, food, and water.

September 1, 2005

Evacuation of the Superdome to Houston's Astrodome is under way; top federal officials deny knowledge of conditions at the Convention Center.

September 2, 2005

Supplies finally arrive at the Convention Center; President Bush approves $10.5 billion in aid.

September 3, 2005

Superdome evacuation is complete; Convention Center evacuation begins; thousands of additional National Guard troops are dispatched to the region.

September 4, 2005

Texas starts moving some of its 250,000 evacuees to other states; 17th Street Canal levee breaches are closed, and the job of pumping water out of the city begins.

September 5, 2005

Mayor Nagin orders remaining residents to leave New Orleans.

September 9, 2005

Congress passes another $51.8 billion in emergency aid; FEMA chief Michael Brown is removed as head of relief operations.

September 15, 2005

Mayor Nagin allows some residents to return to New Orleans.

September 19, 2005

Mayor Nagin orders another evacuation as Hurricane Rita moves into the Gulf of Mexico.

September 24, 2005

Michael Brown and DHS director Michael Chertoff testify before a U.S. Senate committee on the government's response to Katrina.

February 23, 2006

The White House releases a report that addresses mistakes and makes 125 recommendations to improve emergency response.

February 28, 2006

New Orleans celebrates its first Mardi Gras since the hurricane.

ON THE WEB

For more information on *Hurricane Katrina*, use FactHound.

1 Go to *www.facthound.com*

2 Type in this book ID: 0756521017

3 Click on the *Fetch It* button. FactHound will find Web sites related to this book.

HISTORIC SITES

Jean Lafitte National Park and Preserve
419 Decatur St.
New Orleans, LA 70130-1035
504/589-2636

Exhibits and walking tours on the history of New Orleans' French Quarter

The Ogden Museum of Southern Art
University of New Orleans
925 Camp St.
New Orleans, LA
504/539-9600

Collection includes photographs and stories of Hurricane Katrina survivors as well as general artwork documenting the history and culture of Louisiana and other Gulf Coast states

LOOK FOR MORE BOOKS IN THIS SERIES

The Collapse of the Soviet Union:
The End of an Empire
ISBN 0-7565-2009-6

Miranda v. Arizona:
The Rights of the Accused
ISBN 0-7565-2008-8

The Little Rock Nine:
Struggle for Integration
ISBN 0-7565-2011-8

The New Deal:
Rebuilding America
ISBN 0-7565-2096-7

McCarthyism:
The Red Scare
ISBN 0-7565-2007-X

Watergate:
Scandal in the White House
ISBN 0-7565-2010-X

A complete list of **Snapshots in History** titles is available on our Web site: *www.compasspointbooks.com*

Glossary

apocalyptic
involving the most severe destruction imaginable

arsonists
people who intentionally and illegally set property on fire

bureaucracy
strict and complicated regulations, often blamed for slow or illogical government action

catastrophic
extremely damaging

Coast Guard
the branch of the U.S. military that is responsible for defending the coast, protecting people and property at sea, and enforcing customs, immigration, and navigation laws

erosion
the gradual wearing away of soil by water and wind

evacuee
a person who has been moved away from a dangerous situation

hurricane
a severe tropical storm with heavy rains and fast winds that rotate in a wide, counterclockwise circle

looters
people who steal from stores or houses during a time of chaos

Mardi Gras
the last day of Carnival, a two-week celebration that includes parades, parties, and feasts

National Guard
a voluntary military organization with units in each state, usually under the control of the state's governor but available to the president in times of war or emergency

parish
the word used in Louisiana to describe sections of land that would be called counties in other states

red tape
official procedures that are time-consuming and sometimes unnecessary

sludge
a wet, muddy mixture

storm surge
a huge wave of water pushed ashore by an approaching hurricane

Tornado Alley
the middle section of the United States where tornadoes are most common

tsunami
an enormous ocean wave caused by an underwater earthquake or volcanic eruption

Source Notes

Chapter 1:

Page 8, line 12: Susan M. Moyer, ed. *Katrina: Stories of Rescue, Recovery and Rebuilding in the Eye of the Storm.* Champaign, Ill.: Spotlight Press, 2005, p. 22.

Page 11, line 5: Joseph B. Treaster, and Abby Goodnough. "Powerful Storm Threatens Havoc Along Gulf Coast." *The New York Times* 29 Aug. 2005.

Page 11, line 12: "Superdome Provides Shelter, but Not Comfort." FoxNews.com. 29 Aug. 2005. 21 April 2006. www.foxnews.com/story/0,2933,167313,00.html

Page 12, line 20: Ibid.

Page 12, line 27: Aaron Sharockman. "In the Superdome, Thousands Without the Means to Leave." *St. Petersburg Times* 28 Aug. 2005.

Chapter 2:

Page 16, line 14: Joel K. Burne Jr. "Gone with the Water." *NationalGeographic.com* Oct. 2004. 21 April 2006. http://magma.nationalgeographic.com/ngm/0410/feature5/?fs=www3.nationalgeographic.com

Page 20, sidebar: "Washing Away." *The Times-Picayune* June 2002: 23–27.

Chapter 3:

Page 26, line 7: "New Orleans Braces for the Big One." CNN.com. 28 Aug. 2005. 21 April 2006. www.cnn.com/2005/WEATHER/08/28/katrina.neworleans/index.html

Page 28, sidebar: "Hurricane Katrina." National Hurricane Center. 28 Aug. 2005. 22 April 2006. www.nhc.noaa.gov/archive/2005/pub/al122005.public.024.shtml

Chapter 4:

Page 34, line 24: Kathleen Johnston. "Staff at New Orleans Hospital Debated Euthanizing Patients." CNN.com. 13 Oct. 2005. 21 April 2006. www.cnn.com/2005/US/10/12/katrina.hospital/index.html?section=cnn_topstories

Page 36, sidebar: *A Failure of Initiative: Final Report of the Select Bipartisan Committee to Investigate the Preparation and Response to Hurricane Katrina.* U.S. House of Representatives. 15 Feb. 2006, p. 6. 21 April 2006. http://a257.g.akamaitech.net/7/257/2422/15feb20061230/www.gpoaccess.gov/katrinareport/investigation.pdf

Page 38, line 25: "FEMA Chief: Victims Bear Some Responsibility." CNN.com. 1 Sept. 2005. 22 April 2006. www.cnn.com/2005/WEATHER/09/01/katrina.fema.brown

Page 39, line 4: "Meet the Press: Transcript for September 4." MSNBC.com. 4 Sept. 2005. 21 April 2006. www.msnbc.msn.com/id/9179790

Page 40, line 3: "Gunfire Halts Superdome Exodus." KUTV.com. 1 Sept. 2005. 21 April 2006. http://kutv.com/topstories/topstories_story_244091619.html

Page 41, line 5: Julian Borger. "Flood Took Disaster's Agency by Surprise." *The Observer* 4 Sept. 2005.

Page 41, line 9: "President Arrives in Alabama, Briefed on Hurricane Katrina." The White House. Sept. 2005. 21 April 2006. www.whitehouse.gov/news/releases/2005/09/20050902-2.html

Chapter 5:

Page 45, line 1: Audra D.S. Burch. "Among the Ruins, Young Hero Emerges." *The Seattle Times* 2 Sept. 2005.

Page 45, line 14: John Harlow. "Teenager Snatches Bus to Save Dozens." *The Sunday Times* 4 Sept. 2005.

Page 49, sidebar, all: Forum. WDSU.com. 2005–2006. 21 April 2006. www.wdsu.com/news/4918877/detail.html

Page 51, line 3: Debbie Elliott. "NYPD Returns a Favor to Louisiana." NPR.org. 11 Sept. 2005. 21 April 2006. www.npr.org/templates/story/story.php?storyId=4841509

Page 51, line 21: Maria Russell. "The First Time I Really Felt Hope." MSNBC.com. 3 Nov. 2005. 21 April 2006. http://risingfromruin.msnbc.com/2005/11/the_first_time_.html

Page 53, sidebar: "Calling Katrina Survivors 'Refugees' Stirs Debate." MSNBC.com. 7 Sept. 2005. 21 April 2006. www.msnbc.msn.com/id/9232071/" \t "_blank

Page 53, line 21: Jackie Northam. "Katrina Chaos: A Black Eye for U.S. Image?" NPR.org. 21 Sept. 2005. 21 April 2006. www.npr.org/templates/story/story.php?storyId=4857135

Chapter 6:

Page 56, sidebar: "Minnesota Man Offers Homeless Family a Home." Kare11.com. 3 Sept. 2005. 21 April 2006. www.kare11.com/news/news_article.aspx?storyid=106106

Page 59, line 1: Susan Saulny. "Putting Down New Roots in More Solid Ground." *The New York Times* 7 Sept. 2005.

Page 59, line 14: "Making Friends at a New School." CBSNews.com. 7 Sept. 2005. 22 April 2006. www.cbsnews.com/stories/2005/09/07/earlyshow/contributors/melindamurphy/main821737.shtml

Source Notes

Page 63, line 4: Johanna Neuman. "The Land of 10,770 Empty Trailers." *The Los Angeles Times* 10 Feb. 2006.

Chapter 7:

Page 69, line 28: Elizabeth Shogren. "Katrina Stirs Up Issue of Lead in Soil." NPR.org. 1 March 2006. 22 April 2006. www.npr.org/templates/story/story.php?storyId=5240033

Page 70, sidebar: "Video Shows Bush Got Explicit Katrina Warning." MSNBC.com. 2 March 2006. 22 April 2006. http://msnbc.msn.com/id/11627394/

Chapter 8:

Page 77, sidebar: "Dean: U.S. Must Face 'Ugly Truth' About Katrina." CNN.com. 8 Sept. 2005. 22 April 2006. www.cnn.com/2005/POLITICS/09/08/katrina.dean/index.html" \t "_blank

Page 77, line 19: *A Failure of Initiative: Final Report of the Select Bipartisan Committee to Investigate the Preparation and Response to Hurricane Katrina*, p.2

Page 78, line 8: "Transcripts." CNN.com. 23 Feb. 2006. 22 April 2006. http://transcripts.cnn.com/TRANSCRIPTS/0602/23/lol.02.html

Page 79, line 12: Jackie Shafer. "The Case Against Rebuilding the Sunken City of New Orleans." Slate.com 7 Sept. 2005. 22 April 2006. www.slate.com/?id=2125810

Page 80, line 5: "Louisiana Governor: 'We Will Rebuild.'" CNN.com. 15 Sept. 2005. 22 April 2006. www.cnn.com/2005/US/09/14/katrina.impact

Page 81, line 11: Peter Whoriskey. "Post-Katrina Rebuilders Hug Ground, Trust Levees." *The Washington Post* 26 Feb. 2006, p. A03.

Page 81, line 18: Ibid.

Page 83, line 3: Haya El Nasser. "Vision: Rebuild 'New Urban' Mississippi Coast." *USA Today* 11 Oct. 2005.

Page 84, line 16: Ronald Brownstein. "Floodwaters Lift Poverty Debate into Political Focus." *Los Angeles Times* 13 Sept. 2005.

SELECT BIBLIOGRAPHY

"Hurricane Katrina." CNN.com. 2005. 22 April 2006. www.cnn.com/SPECIALS/2005/katrina

"Hurricanes' Aftermath." MSNBC.com. 22 April 2006. www.msnbc.msn.com/id/9107338/

Knauer, Kelly, ed. *Hurricane Katrina: The Storm That Changed America.* New York: Time Inc., 2005.

Moyer, Susan M., ed. *Katrina: Stories of Rescue, Recovery and Rebuilding in the Eye of the Storm.* Champaign, Ill.: Spotlight Press, 2005.

Treaster, Joseph G., and Abby Goodnough. "Powerful Storm Threatens Havoc Along Gulf Coast." *The New York Times* 29 Aug. 2005.

U.S. House of Representatives. *A Failure of Initiative: Final Report of the Select Bipartisan Committee to Investigate the Preparation and Response to Hurricane Katrina.* 15 Feb. 2005. 21 April 2006. http://katrina.house.gov/index.htm

The White House. *The Federal Response to Hurricane Katrina: Lessons Learned.* 23 Feb. 2006. 22 April 2006. http://www.whitehouse.gov/reports/katrina-lessons-learned

"Washing Away." *The Times-Picayune* 23–27 June 2002.

FURTHER READING

Hollingsworth Gessler, Diana. *Very New Orleans: A Celebration of History, Culture, and Cajun Country Charm.* Chapel Hill, N.C.: Algonquin Books of Chapel Hill, 2005.

Lantier-Sampon, Patricia. *Louisiana.* Milwaukee, Wis.: Gareth Stevens, 2006.

Miller, Debra A. *Hurricane Katrina: Devastation on the Gulf Coast.* Farmington Hills, Mich.: Thomson Gale, 2006.

Miller, Mara. *Hurricane Katrina Strikes the Gulf Coast: Disaster and Survival.* Berkeley Heights, N.J.: Enslow Publishers, 2006.

Index